Reclaiming Our Affirmations

A 30 Day Renewal

A Book. A Journal. A Journey.

Jayde C. Ware
Dr. Kellie M. Dixon

Reclaiming Our Affirmations: A 30 Day Renewal
Copyright © 2020 by Jayde C. Ware and Kellie M. Dixon

Printed in the United States of America
First Printing, 2020

ISBN 978-0-578-71193-5 (paperback)

Cover by Tyler A. Williams (www.williamswrites.com)

Dedication

for our grandmothers…and their prayers that served as a GPS when we lost our way

Geraldine C. Dixon (Dr. K's paternal Grandmother)
Martha C. Brown (Dr. K's maternal Grandmother)
Alma Louise Becker (Jayde's maternal Grandmother)
Lelia Mae Harris (Jayde's paternal Grandmother)

Foreword

Not often do I find myself reading a book that speaks to my soul and propels me to grow within the first few pages, but without a doubt *Reclaiming Our Affirmations* does just that.

Of the numerous strategies I have employed on my journey towards self-actualization, self-care, especially affirmation work, has been my greatest tool.

Self-care, or the intentional act of nurturing one's physical, spiritual, and emotional self, is a journey. Not the occasional nail appointment or trip to the movies, but self-care is a compassionate, reflective, and intentional process. Although most of us recognize the value in nurturing ourselves, it is quite often that we overlook our personal needs. Furthermore, because Black Women are championed as "Super Woman" for everyone else, we may neglect the very life-giving practices that can keep us whole. The pressure to succeed is at times all-consuming, leaving the work of self-care undone. We find ourselves struggling to believe we are worthy of living a life without limits. Then, when what we believe about ourselves becomes our reality the result is that we feel stuck. Until we can change our thoughts, we can't change our lives.

Thankfully, there is hope.

Reclaiming Our Affirmations serves as a powerful self-care guide to healing using simple, personal, aspirational truths. While affirmations do not have to be perfect, nor do they have to be another item on our endless checklist of things "to get right", actively engaging in affirmation work *is* a choice. In reading this book, you are deciding to begin the sacred practice of reframing your thoughts. You will be drawn to think differently and be encouraged to "show up" beyond your perceived limitations.

Between the pages of this deeply vulnerable book are raw and lived experiences of two women affirming their worth, redefining what it means to be successful, and challenging themselves to show up boldly.

There is a powerful synergy between Kellie and Jayde that you can tangibly feel throughout *Reclaiming Our Affirmations*, and after observing their journey, I am grateful they decided to bring the rest of us along for the ride.

I should warn you, embracing the authenticity of self can be a struggle, but in the struggle, the truth can be revealed. If our truth is that we need to rest, we must permit ourselves to do so. If our truth is that we are falling short because of excuses or a lack of personal accountability, then we must as Jayde and Kellie declare, put in the work.

I often reveal that the practice of self-care saved my life, but it is perhaps most accurate to say that it was my decision to consistently affirm that I am worthy of living that made all the difference. I am not alone. Each of us has choices to make if we genuinely want to live the lives we deserve. This book is an investment and an AMAZING resource that will help us manifest the power to not just survive but to thrive…Shall we begin?

Respectfully,
Dr. Raé N. Lundy

Introduction

The idea for this book came from a conversation between authors, Jayde and Kellie (Dr. K) back in 2018. To understand how one conversation leads to a book, it's important to know that they have known each other for over 9 years. In that time span their sisterhood has seen and survived a lot of life – so when they sit down to talk, 9 years' worth of knowledge and insight into each other's lives sits down too.

When Reclaiming Our Affirmations was first spoken into the world, Jayde and Kellie (Dr. K) reflected on the moments in which they reclaimed the words spoken over their lives. The two women then made a pact to take on the writing of this book as a consistent 30-day journey. Thirty days because research says it takes 21 to build a habit, but they both knew it would take 30 days to incorporate it as routine. The result is the collection of affirmations on the following pages that will take you on a journey with them, hopefully challenging you to do your own reflecting and journaling along the way.

Before we get to the 30-day journey, I, Queen-Ella Pringle, CEO/Founder of Cornerstone Visionaries Consulting and Coaching, LLC – sat down with Jayde and Kellie (Dr. K) to talk more about the evolution of *Reclaiming Our Affirmations* and wanted to share the conversation with you....

Queen: I'm honored and excited to be sitting with authors Dr. Kellie Dixon and Ms. Jayde Ware on their highly anticipated release of their collaborative book called Reclaiming Our Affirmations. Today, we will get to know the authors and learn more about how Reclaiming Our Affirmations was birthed. Tell us a little about yourselves. Perhaps something not many people know?

Kellie: I am a native of Virginia, born and raised. I am a first generation student, so I am the first of my family to receive an associates, bachelor, master, and doctorate degree. I am a mentor to students and professionals across the world. I am a certified life coach and higher education professional. Something people don't know about me – I love to love, I love hard!

Jayde: I'm also a native of Virginia, even though I have moved pretty often over the last couple years. I began my professional journey in healthcare before realizing dreams change and transitioned to higher education. I now do prevention and health and wellness work with college students. I'm also a writer and a content creator. A not so well kept secret about me is that I love sports and I read a lot!

Queen: Can you tell us about the book *Reclaiming Our Affirmations*? Why 30 days?
Jayde: It's a mix between an affirmation book and a journal. The affirmations go along with certain themes of life – like finding yourself, learning and unlearning, and thoughts that are very raw from our own journals. Research says it takes 21 days to build a habit; however, Kellie and I know it's not just 21 days, but actually 30 days to build consistency. 30 days is the mark when you decide you want to do something different and build it into routine. So in the writing process we dedicated 30 days to sit down and write even when it felt uncomfortable based on the theme for that day.

Queen: I notice your book is dedicated to some very powerful and important women in your lives. Tell us about what influenced that inspiration.
Kellie: This book is dedicated to my paternal and maternal grandmothers. My paternal grandmother passed in 2013 and she always spoke life into me, which was her way of affirming me. This book is dedicated to her for keeping me in prayer and affirming me about my life. And my maternal grandmother, who is still alive, her strength is impeccable. Things that she has endured and how she keeps moving and willing to help or pray for others even in her sickest moments is powerful. Both of their genes are within me and part of the fabric of who I am.
Jayde: I also dedicated this book to my grandmothers. Losing them both has had a profound impact on me. My maternal grandmother battled Alzheimer's disease for years and I felt robbed of so many memories with her due to the disease, which inspired me to go into to healthcare to help other families. My paternal grandmother was and still is my best friend. Her death shook to me my core and was the catalyst for all of the internal work I started doing. They were both outspoken and engrained in me at a young age that our words have power. This book is in a lot of ways one of the promises I'm keeping to them.

Queen: Take us back to how this started. How did you begin working on this together? How long did it take you to write *Reclaiming Our Affirmation book*?
Kellie: When we started writing this 2 years ago, we were both in a space of "we grown, we been waiting to be grown, but isn't no manual for this so what are we doing? There were a lot of stressed days and incident that occurred between us both professionally and personally that we discussed among ourselves. We realized we couldn't be the only ones facing this in

adulthood. So this led to what affirmations we have for ourselves, what do we say to ourselves when we are in good spaces and how do we reclaim those affirmations. However, we put the book down 2 years ago and didn't publish it then.

Jayde: Kellie mentioned putting the book down. I can own that putting the book down was mainly me. There were days when I didn't want to write because I didn't want to sit in my insecurities that day. I was in the thick of them so I just put the book down hoping that maybe one day I'd feel like I could write through it.

Queen: You stated it took 2 years to complete this book, and a few reasons why but did you experience adversity, milestones, or ah ha moments from the time you started writing until now at the time of publishing?

Kellie: Wow, I sit back and think about all I was dealing with and going through personally and professionally. I wish someone had written this book for me at that time, I was lost and no one knew it. So this book is raw and unfiltered because of what I was experiencing during the journey. There were many ah ha moments for sure!

Jayde: When we started writing, we were bringing so much into the book. We were bringing every bag we hadn't unpacked, every insecurity, and every uncomfortable feeling. At this time I was also going through heavy identity work. I tied so much of my identity to my accomplishments, work, and my career but I didn't really know myself. I just knew I was miserable. After many calls to Kellie while sitting under my desk sobbing, she helped me transition out of healthcare and into higher education. I thought this career change was going to fix everything, but it didn't. I was still unsure of myself. Internally, I was a mess – which made writing this book so much harder for me.

Queen: What are Affirmations and benefits of practicing them daily? When did you first realize you wanted to write a book on affirmations? Where did you get your insight for the daily affirmations?

Kellie: The power of your words and what you speak over your life. There are enough people in the world speaking negatively against us and some of us feed into that. Affirmations to me – it's a reminder of saying why I am enough, reminder of why I need self-discipline, reminder of why I need to practice self-love. I am a firm believer in manifestation, so what you speak, will become. When I speak affirmations, it's the key to unlock some doors.

Jayde: Kellie hit it. I believe everything that we say out loud goes into the world and as Kellie said, manifests. So in regards to affirmations, I go back to childhood – before anyone told me I wasn't smart or talented or whatever else… because the world tells us that we're not and can't do a lot of things,

9

but affirmations give us reclaiming powers. Affirmations remind me that I was created from a place of worthiness and I am still worthy. Saying that out loud matters!

Queen: Of the 30-day affirmation, which one resonates with you most today and why?
Kellie: Well, for me its Day 22 – empty out your thoughts and feelings – I divorce self-sabotage and I release the feelings that are not mind to hold. I am at a point now where I can't hold my feelings anymore because they do me no justice, they just consume my mind. I am in a space that is scary to feel now and have it in words to tell someone because it makes me vulnerable. I realize that when I hold on to these feelings, I self-sabotage and miss out on many blessings. Every time Jayde and I talk, she brings up my self-sabotage habits – I am finally listening because I know I have missed the mark because of it. Thank you!
Jayde: Day 25 – "eventually you will have to release all the dreams you caught." In the last 2 years I have spent a lot of time unpacking everything that I was taught. And I finally feel courageous enough to be just who I am. In undergrad I was always protecting this image of who I thought I was supposed to be and then I graduated and the façade shattered. I spent so much of my life being what people told me to be. So much of my adulthood has been unlearning all the things the world told me to be. I've spent years being uncomfortable on my path and then running from that discomfort. I think I'm finally walking in my purpose and I finally understand why God slows us down to lean into the discomfort before we find genuine joy.

Queen: What was the most surprising moment of realization or self-actualization you've experienced while writing your book?
Kellie: I was writing two books at the same time, this one and Recharge – I sat both of them now! I eventually picked up Recharge to complete a few months ago because I had someone who motivated me to finish it and publish. I am still in awe that I became an author. Then, while watching an Instagram concert between Jill Scott and Erykah Badu, Jill said "Once it's on paper, it doesn't even belong to you anymore – you have to release it to the world. It's mandatory." I felt all of this! I immediately texted Jayde and said, it's time to finish and release the book. So going back to writing and editing the book, I entered a space where I believe all the affirmations and I am finally in a place where I can share and receive love, that's my self-actualization. I am ready for everything good that God has for me in my life!
Jayde: Believing that I could actually write the book. I still had this voice in my head saying "Jayde you can't write a book, you write blog posts, you and stuff for social media, but you're not like an author author." I kept obsessing

over how I was going to convince people to read this book – then I finally had this moment where I realized before I could convince people to read my book, first I had to convince myself that I could actually write the book – I needed to start there!

Queen: You both are awe-inspiring! Healing comes in many forms and through candid conversations and digging deep, healing arises. Sometimes you can't have these conversations by yourself and you need someone to pull it out of you in the most gentle and compassionate way. So, how can your readers incorporate these affirmations in their daily lives? What suggestions do you have for your readers who are looking to practice self- care healing?
Kellie: I think it's different for everyone. For me, I am a visual, so I use sticky notes and place them on a mirror in my room. Because I know that in order for me to truly love someone else, I have to love myself. And before I can love myself, I have to like myself. So, visually seeing affirmations and having open candid conversations with people I trust, holds me accountable to my affirmations.
Jayde: I am big on putting things on paper. Every morning, I spend about 15 minutes writing and there's always an affirmation. I also text people affirmations all the time. But like Kellie said – I think it's different for everyone. I need to see it, say it, and have others affirm me. Sometimes even Kellie will speak affirmations over me and I'm like "oh okay Kellie."
Kellie: Iron sharpens iron!

Queen: What's that impact, that legacy you can see from this book?
Kellie: I think it is in the name of the book. You don't always have to have it together – but who said you had to have it all together? As long as you have the opportunity to wake up and breathe, you can reclaim the affirmations that you have told yourself. Like, who defines together – what does it really mean to *have it together*? To – Get – Her! So as long as you moving, you still have the opportunity – there is power in the words we speak. Our words overflow to other people, so we have to be cautious in that too. So the impact, for me, is that we don't lose sight of the present moment. Just because I don't have it together today, doesn't mean I won't have it together tomorrow. But you will never get to tomorrow's mindset, if you don't get through today's mindset. So continue to reclaim. Reclaiming is saying that it is already yours, you are just refreshing it!
Queen: Recharging it!
Jayde: Kellie and I often have these very real conversations with each other. We navigate adulthood and try to make sense of things by talking through them. This is us adding chairs to our table and having conversations about vulnerability, life, and the messiness of adulthood that we are often ashamed

and afraid to talk about – we want others to have these conversations with us.

Queen: I think that will be so instrumental for your readers to sit in that. So where can your readers support you and follow your journey?
Kellie: Well, you can follow me on Twitter (@misskellie_1) and my business page at (@clearpathway) and Instragram (@misskellie_1).
Jayde: You can keep up with Jayde via twitter (@astoldbyjayde) and Instagram (@callherjayde).

Queen: Thank you for taking the opportunity to allow us to join your space and learn more about this extraordinary literary piece called Reclaiming Our Affirmations. There you have it. We embarked on a candid and amazing conversation with Dr. Dixon and Ms. Ware. Now you have the opportunity to start or enhance your own self- awareness, self-encouragement, and self-motivation with the guidance of *Reclaiming Our Affirmations*.

Let the journey begin....

DAY ONE

Acknowledge the work to be done and do it.

I am committed to doing the work.
I know the work will not always be pretty or fun and still choose to do it anyway. I know that everything begins and ends with doing the work.

Jayde's Thoughts

I exist somewhere between relentlessly pursuing my goals and wrapping myself in excuses under the guise of self-care. I have days where I commit 150% to the work and tap into a no excuses – mind over matter – win at all costs mindset. Only to then trudge full force into a place dominated by self-compassion and grace. And while I drench myself in my own kindness here – it also leaves me just enough room to breathe life into excuses for not keeping promises to myself. I struggle to find the balance between one voice yelling "how are you tired when you only gave 30% today? No rest until the goal is reached" and another voice whispering "I know 30% was all you could muster up today and that's okay, rest."

Extending grace is important, but accountability is important too – and accountability can exist without shame. The world will not wait for you, for me, or any of us to be or feel 100% ready to do the work. The world doesn't pay dividends to our excuses. Execution is queen – and she will not badger or beg for your participation. There will never be an alternative route to just doing the damn work.

Kellie's Thoughts

There is a sense of clarity and peace when I write out my plan for the day, week, month, year. I feel liberated and in control of my own journey. I get to decide what the steps are and move at my own pace. Then there is that moment of "now, when do you start." The starting point is always the frustrating part because I use to say "when I get myself together I am going to work this plan". Let's be honest, if we wait until we are "together" we will never make the move. So, I have come to grasp with the simple fact "as long as I am carrying out the plan, I am together". Like many, I assume, I have a million things racing through my head at any given moment. So writing/journaling, practicing mindfulness, and working out has been great to ease my mind, write the plan, and get it done. In order to get to the destination, I have to fuel up the tank, get in the driver seat, and GO!.

MY DAY ONE

"We all have dreams. But in order to make dreams come into reality, it takes an awful lot of determination, dedication, self-discipline, and effort." -Jesse Owens

_____

_____

_____

_____

_____

_____

_____

_____

_____

_____

_____

_____

_____

_____

_____

_____

DAY TWO

Self-discipline is a needed step.

I have the discipline, patience, and passion to achieve all of my goals. My dreams are already my reality. I divorce self-sabotage.

Jayde's Thoughts

Discipline is important, it just isn't fun. It's also hard and doesn't always feel good in the moment, which makes it easy to evade us. You cannot just say you want better and expect better to show up at your doorstep. Dreams don't work without self-restraint. Goals aren't achieved without self-control.

If dreams are the seeds we plant then discipline is the sunlight that breathes life into them. Without sunlight, plants die – and without self-discipline, dreams do too. Discipline starts with a decision. One decision to commit to something. One decision to sacrifice temporary pleasure for what matters long term. Discipline is a commitment to yourself, for yourself - and if you're going to honor any commitments, you should start with the ones you make to yourself.

Kellie's Thoughts

Admitting to yourself that you need to make some serious changes in your life is difficult as hell! Every day, I feel like I have something to work on and find myself looking for clear directions. I would start so many projects and leave them hanging (similar to this book lol). I lacked self-discipline, which in my opinion, is the ignition to getting you on the right path. The path you so desperately want and probably need, if we are being honest. There will always be temptations and distractions, but self-discipline is one hell of an antidote to keep you focused on what's important...you and your goals! The idea of disciplining yourself sounds rude and disrespectful, when I sit and think about it. However, I recognize that no one else will achieve my goals for me. I remove the action and thoughts of getting in my own way. The time is now and living in the moment has been one of the best attributes to understanding and practicing self-discipline for myself.

MY DAY TWO

"Good planning without good working is nothing." - Dwight D. Eisenhower

_____

_____

_____

_____

_____

_____

_____

_____

_____

_____

_____

_____

_____

_____

_____

_____

DAY THREE

You can change the perception about yourself.
Life is for me. All things work on my behalf.
I've already won. I free myself from creating barriers to my own success.

Jayde's thoughts
The great thing is, I have the power at any time to change the story I tell myself about myself. The terrifying thing is, I have the power at any time to change the story I tell myself about myself.

I am a firm believer that every change in our lives happens as a result of us deciding that we have to move differently. Every person we love can tell us we need to change, but until we get tired of our own shit, we will never fully commit to changing. There is magic in the moment we finally realize that who we are today is not who we have to be tomorrow. There's magic in recognizing that at any time we can take our tools and build a new foundation for our lives. There's magic in knowing it's never too late to begin again – and to keep on beginning again until life feels right.

Kellie's thoughts
Everyone seems to create this story of who you are because of your past and even present life experiences and decisions. However, they haven't asked for the facts, yet they still make this story for others to "know" who you are. It's pure nonsense, don't believe the hype. People have versions of who I am. Only I have the facts with explanations (not that I need to explain myself to others). Who I am is at the core of my existence and somehow I have allowed society and people to throw their manuscripts of my life over me, but their time is up and their story won't be published. This is me, flaws and all. Have I made mistakes, plenty! Yet, my life is for me and no one can write the script like me. Sometimes, others perceptions of you are tied to their own insecurities. Just saying- think about it! My life is for my purpose and as long as I honor God's calling over my life, I walk boldly.

MY DAY THREE

"Don't spend your life believing a story about yourself that you didn't write that's been fed to you." - Rasheed Ogunlaru

_____

_____

_____

_____

_____

_____

_____

_____

_____

_____

_____

_____

_____

_____

_____

_____

DAY FOUR

You aren't lost, stop finding yourself and start appreciating yourself.

I am my own answered prayers.
I already am everything I want.

Jayde's Thoughts

Last summer I went on solo road trip that spanned several states in an effort to find myself. A violent downpour forced me to pull over on a backroad in Memphis where I was forced to come face to face with myself. I sat silently half afraid of being on the side of the road in a strange place and half paralyzed by the realization that I was in the car by myself and was still traveling with a stranger. That time spent sitting by myself led to one of the most important "AHA!" moments of my life.

I realized that I didn't need to find myself after all, that I was still there... that underneath all of the identities I adopted over the years was still the 7 year old girl who ran to her mama when life knocked her down and the 12 year old who cried when B2K broke up, and even the timid 19 year old who only spoke when forced. I was still the over-involved over-achiever who obsessed over detail or every small thing and beat herself up when perfection couldn't be obtained. That I had been there this entire time, just begging to be accepted.

Maybe in the moments we think we've lost ourselves, it's really just a signal to ourselves to come back home to ourselves. Maybe feeling lost is us begging to be loved for who we are at our core... you know the version of ourselves that were just free, until someone somewhere told us we had to be something else.

Kellie's Thoughts

As I sit in tears writing this, I have spent my whole life "finding myself". Because I wasn't the most beautiful, the most sought after, at least in my eyes (which mattered the most), I thought I was irrelevant, lost, because no one saw me. I DIDN'T SEE ME. I dreamed constantly about who I wanted to be and what I needed to do; however, it was a struggle to be this person. What I didn't realize was, I was already her. I just needed to peel back the layers and appreciate the young girl and now woman standing in front of me each day. The song that resonates to me the most in regards to appreciating myself is "I'm Here" from The Color Purple soundtrack.

"I believe I have inside of me. Everything that I need to live a bountiful life. And all the love alive in me. I'll stand as tall as the tallest tree. And I'm thankful for every day that I'm given. Both the easy and hard ones. I'm livin'. But most of all, I'm thankful for. Lovin' who I really am. I'm beautiful. Yes, I'm beautiful. And I'm here!"

MY DAY FOUR

"I think you travel to search and you come back home to find yourself there." - Chimamanda Ngozi Adichie

_____

_____

_____

_____

_____

_____

_____

_____

_____

_____

_____

_____

_____

DAY FIVE

Competency is not about age, yet experiences.

I have all I need in this moment; God has equipped me with all that I need. I am wise enough, smart enough, and strong enough to do this. I deserve to be here in this space. I deserve all of the abundance in my life.

Jayde's Thoughts

"If I needed something more, I'd have it; a seat was created for me at this table because I add value, I am needed here." Phrases I find myself repeating often. I made these daily reminders after I grew exhausted of losing battles to imposter syndrome. My professional life has yielded me a lot of positions and titles I haven't always felt qualified for. I've been deemed an expert, a director, a manager and put in charge of creating companywide protocols – and yet, I still have to convince myself of my own competence sometimes.

Imposter syndrome will sway me to believe that someone will eventually knock on my office door and say "aye, you can stop fronting now" and walk me smooth out the front door. It tells me things like 'I'm too much of this, not enough that', or that 'I'm lacking some credential to be worthy enough to be here'. It never says I'm not capable, it just relentlessly whispers things like "you're not supposed to be here yet" and tells me "there's a hundred other people who should be here instead." While it's hard not to fixate on these whispers, I'm learning that experience doesn't need age to qualify you because it stands on its own. And sometimes we're given the tools to do the important work before we even know what the work is – and even when imposter syndrome sinks its teeth in me, I still add value and I am still worthy.

Kellie's Thoughts

I am just in awe of the simplicity in knowing that my experiences serve as a foundation for my future. Age has nothing to do with that. Everyone, at every age experiences life differently and reacts accordingly. I grew up believing that the older I got the smarter I would be and I knew nothing because I was young. I am glad that the older I got the wiser I became. I may not have known a lot intellectually; however, my experiences at a young age taught me a lot about what I am dealing with now. If I didn't know it, better believe an experience was right around the corner to supply me with what I needed. Competency is about your ability to do something. There are individuals much younger than me with competencies I can't begin to process on my own (lol). Take every day experiences to build up your competencies. Yes, some things you have to wait until you are "of age" (whatever that really means), otherwise, live on!

MY DAY FIVE
"Be careful not to mistake early incompetency as inherent weakness." - Jamie Arpin-Ricci

_____

_____

_____

_____

_____

_____

_____

_____

_____

_____

_____

_____

DAY SIX

Be genuine in your need, ask for help.

I trust myself and God to have my back.
The Universe will provide.
I don't have to do it all alone.

Jayde's Thoughts

Being brave enough to seek out help is a form of vulnerability – and well, my relationship with vulnerability is a volatile one. I've always considered vulnerability the first cousin of weakness – and I never wanted to be seen as weak. This fear of weakness paved the way for me to fit the strong friend role. It also smacked my hand every time I tried to take the cape off to admit I couldn't do it all alone either.

I've had to lay down the armor and learn that is safe to admit I struggle too. I've had to learn how to be vulnerable enough to ask for help – and I've had to open myself to receiving help. But, most importantly I've had to unlearn everything that told me bravery and seeking helping could not coexist. There is power in being brave enough to say "I don't have all the answers, I need some help," and actually opening yourself up to receive it.

Kellie's Thoughts

At the age of 32, I scheduled my first therapy session with a licensed counselor. As an educated woman with a degree in counseling and a certified life coach, I thought I was good. Hell, if I can be there for others and help them through the toughest time, then I must be great, right? That is far from the truth, I struggle and it wasn't until 2-3 years ago prior that I became vocal about it (with a select few) because there is that stigma about mental health and the Black community. When you are always seen as the one to "have it together", you allow that to be your pseudo truth, in my opinion. However, there is that moment when you sit alone and say "if people really knew how I showed up when no one was around". I no longer feel the need to fake it or cover it up. I need help! With God, self-care techniques, and counseling, I will be good, so sign me up! Remember, even the giver needs to be replenished to give more! I admit, I battle with depression and adjustment disorders. Whew, there is it is...I am not always okay; however, I am always well – I recognize the difference!

MY DAY SIX

"The strong individual is the one who asks for help when [s]he needs it" - Rona Barrett

---

DAY SEVEN

Too many people will cause self-neglect if you aren't careful.

I am enough on my own. I am at the top of my priority list. I recognize I cannot be everything to everyone and I free myself any guilt that comes with that.

Jayde's Thoughts

The hardest part of my journey has been healing my quiet and obscure insecurities. Insecurities that present themselves as: wanting to be everything to everybody, overextending myself because I don't want to disappoint anyone, and needing to be needed. Therapy has taught me those insecurities stem from all the years I never felt like I belonged anywhere, so my defense mechanism became the art of morphing into this superwoman ideal.

Superwoman said "yes" to every ask and sacrificed her own well-being to make things happen. She walked 3 miles when someone only asked for 1. She was always there with hands ready to help – and she was on top of the world. Until superwoman, me, was depleted of resources. I spent so much time giving to everyone else that I forgot to take care of home, first.

Self-sacrifice isn't a badge of honor. It's labor that doesn't pay or even come with benefits. If you want to fully walk in your purpose, you have to consistently give yourself your full attention too.

Kellie's Thoughts

I have sacrificed enough of who I am and want to be for others sake. No more, that way of living is over. I realized that everyone will have an opinion about your life, whether you doing good, bad, or indifferent. It is enough going on in the world to have to be surrounded by people that don't understand your growth and the process needed to get to where you want to be. "Too much focus on the quantity takes away from the value of the quality - this is my motto for the people in and around my 'circle'. When your circle is small you are able to manage yourself and how you show up better, which lessens the room for self-neglect. I can no longer stretch myself thin to make others happy. I have to validate my own happiness, cause when the lights are out, it's just me and my reflection. I reclaim my time from the people who didn't honor it.

MY DAY SEVEN

"Don't chase people. Be yourself, do your own thing and work hard. The right people - the ones who really belong in your life - will come to you And stay." - Will Smith

_____

_____

_____

_____

_____

_____

_____

_____

_____

_____

_____

_____

_____

_____

_____

DAY EIGHT

Others expectations of me don't fit my experiences. Live life!

I free myself from the expectations others have placed on me. I give myself permission to grow beyond the boxes other people have put me in. I recognize that I am not the expectations I fall short of.

Jayde's Thoughts

I've mastered the art of shapeshifting to fit whatever box people's expectations put me in. I carefully crafted every word to avoid being too controversial and making even a tiny wave. This made me likable and likable fits in boxes like a glove. The only problem with contorting myself to be likable enough to fit every box? Even with me in them, they were still empty.

I had to unlearn the patterns that made shrinking into boxes seem safer than showing up as my authentic self. I had to give myself permission to fall short of the expectations I never agreed to adopt as my own. I had to free myself of the guilt I felt for disappointing people. And it has been a battle every step of the way – but fighting to release myself from expectations that aren't mine to hold is nothing compared to the hell of not showing up in this world as my authentic self.

Kellie's Thoughts

For the majority of my life, I have lived my life based on others definitions of success and their expectations of what they thought was best for me. This is an easy trap to fall into when you are not clear of your purpose and passions in life. However, you don't have to stay in this trap. Understanding your WHY for life, your purpose, is critical to defining your own expectations and not relying on those set by others. I believe people's expectations of you are simply to benefit them and not you. You operate on their schedule. Yeah, that's played out as of now and will never come back in style. I am a firm believer in only expecting people to show up just as they are. As for me, I understand my purpose and the expectations others have set for me has no bearing in me achieving my goals. My experiences are not the same as yours, so stop expecting me to react and respond like you. There are different ways to get to similar destination points. Let me live and speak my own testimony!

MY DAY EIGHT

"I have learned that as long as I hold fast to my beliefs and values – and follow my own moral compass – then the only expectations I need to live up to are my own" – Michelle Obama

_____

_____

_____

_____

_____

_____

_____

_____

_____

_____

_____

_____

_____

_____

DAY NINE

People will remix your life and never give recognition to the original.

I recognize that my life is magic.
I am the secret ingredient; I am the magic touch.

Jayde's Thoughts

One of my favorite quotes is "no can be you and that is your superpower." It affirms everything I believe about authenticity and showing up as yourself being the secret sauce to success. There is power in knowing that you are the magic behind your success, you are the secret ingredient. You always have been and you always will be.

Kellie's Thoughts

There is only one me; therefore, you could never be better than me. In order to be better than me, you would first have to be me and that will not happen. My competition is me yesterday vs me today. Full of struggles, flaws, scars, tears, victories, beauty, and success...my life is magical. The more transparent I am about my life, the more accountable I am towards my life mission and how it is recognized by others. There is not enough pixie dust to compliment the magical life I get to live daily. I am the ONE and ONLY narrator and NO ONE can ever remix or disregard the originality of my journey. I refuse to give people such perceived power to do so. God has given us all a measure of gifts and talents – I honr Him for my portion and you should do the same!

MY DAY NINE

"Sometimes, I feel discriminated against, but it does not make me angry. It merely astonishes me. How can any deny themselves the pleasure of my company? It's beyond me." – Zora Neale Hurston

_____

_____

_____

_____

_____

_____

_____

_____

_____

_____

_____

_____

_____

_____

_____

DAY TEN

Regroup and refocus.

I give myself permission to let go of the things that no longer serve me. I free myself from the relationships, environments, and beliefs that no longer serve me.

Jayde's Thoughts

I like endings. I believe they're powerful and necessary. Endings signal completed lessons and rebirth in a sense. They allow us to reassess where we're spending our energy and make better investments. They free us. Endings untie our hands and our lives to ensure we have full ability to make room for the next level.

I think every level up involves some sort of ending that makes way for newness. Teaching us that sometimes letting go is an act of grace and love too. After all, it's hard to cultivate new habits when your focus is still out back playing with all those things God told you to put down.

Kellie's Thoughts

Its Day 10, as a learner of numbers and their meanings, 10 means the completion of a cycle. On this day, the cycle of hoarding unneeded relationships and things is done. Let go and keep moving! I make no apologies for letting go of people and things that no longer serve me. In order to live freely of negativity, I must first recognize the barriers in my life (whether they are their voluntarily or involuntarily). Demi Lovato's song "You Don't Do It for Me Anymore" is a testament to this process of regrouping and refocusing your time and energy. You should check it out. Meanwhile, recharging is a thing (I wrote a whole book about my method for recharging and achieving your goals through a self-awareness approach). You have to know when you are out of alignment, when you need a "tune up". Stop walking through life unaligned and "faking it until I make it" – it is not becoming of me nor you. Let's regroup and refocus and take inventory of what and who is in our life.

MY DAY TEN
"You can't always trust people who you once thought saved you" - Demi Lovato

_____

_____

_____

_____

_____

_____

_____

_____

_____

_____

_____

_____

_____

_____

_____

DAY ELEVEN

Every day is an opportunity. You decide whether it will be bad or good.

I divorce the idea that I am unworthy of love. I create sunshine wherever I go. I have the power to create the life I want.

Jayde's Thoughts

Like we can change the stories we tell ourselves, we can decide what we take from every experience.

I am not foolishly optimistic or inherently pleasant. I have my shit. I have days where all the bad unpacks at my front door and I sink into it. Followed by days of bouncing back. I have moments where hope dangles in front of me, reminding that no matter where I am, there will always be good there too. I believe in the power of good. I believe that even bad experiences bring new opportunities to life. And even days filled with let downs, rejections, and closed doors are essential for dreams to come to fruition.

Kellie's Thoughts

Every day I am able to wake up, I am reminded of just how blessed I am. The breath I take, the movement of my limbs, and my voice is all I need to make the best of any situation that is presented to me. I know that despite any obstacle, I am loved by others and most importantly, I LOVE ME! The people who love me want me to be happy and I don't have to be a certain way for them to show their love. I have the tools to create the life I want; I just need to make the decisions! Life experiences happen and I have to admit, some have changed my outlook on life...but it doesn't keep me away from taking on opportunities that matter most to me. However, I recognize my stubbornness in some decisions and indecisive mindset at times....I mean I am a Virgo (lol). I have learned (and still learning) to LIVE IN THE MOMENT!

MY DAY ELEVEN

"In every day, there are 1,440 minutes. That mean we have 1,440 daily opportunities to make a positive impact" - Les Brown

_____

_____

_____

_____

_____

_____

_____

_____

_____

_____

_____

_____

_____

_____

_____

DAY TWELVE

This moment is all there is. Own it.

I give myself permission to acknowledge my fears; I am courageous enough to face them head on. I know there is power in my attention and I give my full attention to this moment.

Jayde's Thoughts

I've spent a lot of time not really living because I was trapped by fear. I was always "too" something – too afraid to leap if I couldn't see the ground clearly, too focused on planning to actually execute, too busy worrying about tomorrow to enjoy today, and too busy trying to be this image of perfect to just be myself. But mainly, I was so fixated on a moment which hadn't even arrived yet, that I forgot the current one was a gift too.

When you live a life of always planning for the next win, you deprive yourself the opportunity to celebrate the wins of right now. Year 27 taught me that. It also taught me that sometimes you have to tuck away your fears to make the most out of this moment. This moment is all there ever really is. You have now. Move, do, act, create now.

Kellie's Thoughts

So pouring from Day 11, still embracing the concept to *live in the moment*. I owe it to myself to LIVE and not EXIST, I know my days are numbered! If I continue to allow fear to dictate my life, then what life am I living. I have allowed myself to acknowledge that which I can control and what I cannot. The practice of mindfulness has been a major influence in my life over the 2017. Mindfulness has allowed me to live more presently, to "be where my feet are". I find myself meditating more and especially at times when my anxiety is high. I am still learning and finding my way; however, mindfulness is powerful and beneficial for holistic well-being.

MY DAY TWELVE

"If you want to conquer fear, don't sit home and think about it. Go out and get busy" - Dale Carnegie

DAY THIRTEEN

Move now, later may never come.

I deserve to be here in this space. I deserve all of the abundance in my life.

Jayde's Thoughts

My journals from June 2018 – when we first started this journey and when I decided to trade my healthcare unit director position in for an entry level higher education position:

- The longer you wait, the harder it is to actually do it – whatever "it" may be.
- It's easy to say that you'll do that thing someday – but someday isn't a day that can be counted on.
- Most people are afraid to be beginners, but every master of their craft was once a beginner too.
- It doesn't matter how talented you are or how much potential you have if you just sit on that talent and potential forever.
- There will never be a check to be deposited for all talk and no follow through.
- Perfectionism will convince us we have to do everything perfect, so much so we won't even trust ourselves to take the first step.

Kellie's Thoughts

Every space I occupy, whether in my mind or physically, is for me. I deserve to move with grace and abundance. It is not by accident that I walk into certain spaces in my life. And with each space I occupy, I know there is an opportunity for a lesson to be taught. I know God is preparing me for what I have prayed for! Even through the struggles and dark tunnels, there is still a light that guides me toward my vision. I embrace the good, bad, and indifferent because without it, there is no story, no testimony to inspire someone else. And in every space, there is a *PACE* that only I understand. So yes, I am here to take up MY space. I deserve to be here!

MY DAY THIRTEEN

"If you believe you deserve better, you will create better for yourself." - Dr. Phil McGraw

_____

_____

_____

_____

_____

_____

_____

_____

_____

_____

_____

_____

_____

_____

_____

DAY FOURTEEN

I don't have to be perfect.

I know I don' have to perform in order to be loved. I know that I am enough on my own. I release the fear of being judged for being me. I free myself from needing someone else to recognize my brilliance.

Jayde's Thoughts

Perfectionism:

- has taught us that we should always be waiting for the perfect time or moment or season – and while we're busy waiting, people and opportunities move on without us.
- is a crutch.
- does not make us more or less worthy of love; we are worthy of love just by being.
- is a master at distraction. It will tell you that you can't release your ideas, art, and work into the world because it's not perfect.
- is something I realize I cannot attain and I give myself grace to be okay with that.

Kellie's Thoughts

I am perfectly IMPERFECT and that's just perfect! Spent many years living in the shadows of others because I didn't understand my own worth, nor truth. Everyone surrounding me had so much more to offer and I believed that. I truly believed it, that I was nothing alone. I felt like others had to validate me! I found myself doing things so that others would recognize me. I wanted people to see me – however I didn't like the attention when it came. In order to live healthy, I must commit to who I am, unapologetically – here is my finding and owning my truth. I don't move unless God tells me to, so I release the fear of being judged by others. Frankly, if God is satisfied and continues to bless me accordingly – then why am I concerned about your reactions? To every person that has judged me and will judge me, I rule it a MISTRIAL! I am both guilty and innocent of a lot of things, yet most importantly, I don't need a defense lawyer or anyone else to speak on my behalf. My truth is a reflection of my works and not your perception of who I am and who I am supposed to be. Miss me with that bull ----!

MY DAY FOURTEEN

"I made decisions that I regret, and I took them as learning experiences. I'm human, not perfect, like anybody else" - Queen Latifah

DAY FIFTEEN

Be better than the person you were yesterday, that's your only competition.

Greatness has been in me all along.

Jayde's Thoughts

If you think you're doing better than the peers you're wasting time comparing yourself to, but you are only tapping into 80% of your potential, you are still taking an L. I know because I've been there. I've had times where I appeared to be lapping my peers in some imaginary career competition I made up in my head, only to discover I was still unfulfilled. Social media will have you turning everything into a competition if you're not intentional.

If you have an urge to be and do better, let it be intentional. If you're going to measure progress, let it be up against your own. We all know competition requires that you dig deep and demand more from yourself to be better – if you're going to demand more, let it be from yourself. And not an illusion of keeping up with and competing against people who don't even know they're competing in the first place.

Kellie's Thoughts

Competing against yourself is hard as hell! I just have to be real frank with that. To know my every move and to 'lose' from time to time is frustrating. As an athlete, I know that feeling both on and off the court. You watch tapes of opponents to prep for a game, you practice, and you still walk away with the "L". However, I keep getting up and going to compete another day. I have learned to appreciate the simple fact that "a win does not ensure praise and a loss does not define defeat". At times, I have found that with every win there is always someone or something reminding me that I could have done better. On the other hand, a lost is just more ambition to keep fighting. Whether I win or lose the competition against myself, I still discover new ways to achieve more on the next day. "As long as you are on the team, you have the opportunity to be better, even if you are on the bench".

MY DAY FIFTEEN
"Turned all my L's into lessons" - Chance The Rapper

_____

_____

_____

_____

_____

_____

_____

_____

_____

_____

_____

_____

_____

_____

_____

_____

DAY SIXTEEN

Remember, it's a marathon, not a sprint.

I recognize my power and I am ready to fully walk in it.

Jayde's Thoughts

Two thoughts at an intersection:

- One does not just get up one morning and decide to run a marathon. You train for it. You make sacrifices daily. You then will yourself to the finish line.
- Your purpose will not require you to race. God's plan for your life does not require to full out sprint to the finish line. Purpose requires pace. Dreams require fierce dedication. I don't believe you can really put a time on that.

I exist somewhere in between both of these thoughts being true at the same time.

Kellie's Thoughts

Yesterday I realized that the person I was aiming to be is not who I need or desire to be any longer. This realization hit harder than anything imaginable. I worked hard, so hard to get to some places. I was racing for time because I had to be something so certain by a particular age. I sacrificed so much free time, family time, and friend time – social well-being. All that just to realize that I didn't want it anymore. As long as you are living in your truth and recognize all your power, you are timeless. Every moment, every second you take - walk in your purpose – PROMISE YOURSELF! Instead of preparing for a long journey, I was building myself up for a quick start and a quick finish. Not anymore. I recognize what I want and need. I appreciate the preparation phases, the patience needed, the endurance to keep moving even when a quicker way is close by. This masterpiece takes time!

MY DAY SIXTEEN

"I think every individual has his or her own power, and it's a matter of working, taking time and defining what that power is" -Jill Scott

---

DAY SEVENTEEN

As long as you are moving, you are taking the next step.

I divorce the idea that I have to settle. I commit to taking the small steps even when I don't know the full way yet.

Jayde's Thoughts

I'm not always courageous, I don't have it all together, I don't always have a plan or a vision of what comes next, and I still have moments of hesitation – but I don't let any of that keep me stuck. I refuse to let the not knowing be an excuse for doing nothing. I trust that even if the next step has some sort of failure attached, that failure will still propel me forward.

Kellie's Thoughts

With all that realization from Day 16, this is the most appropriate follow up! Just because I once wanted to do something, doesn't mean that I have to settle on it. Life allows you to go through many experiences, which shape who you are and who you once thought you were. I have found myself plenty times settling in experiences due to comfort and personally, my fear of success. Yes, it is a real thing to fear success and I have been battling it for a very long time. Because I have spent so much of my life achieving goals others thought were great for me, I defined success by their definition and not my own. It seemed like every time I achieved a level of success by their merits, they had another goal ready. "Oh great, I knew you could do it. I bet now you are going to do this:" And me being me, "oh yeah, I guess so". I didn't want to disappoint them however at the same time I wasn't successful in my eyes, so I remained stagnant for a while. Not anymore. I am not settling for others aspirations of who they believe I should be. I am taking every step I can to discover my joy, my happiness, my success, this is my LEGACY.

MY DAY SEVENTEEN

"If you haven't found it yet, keep looking" - Steve Jobs

DAY EIGHTEEN

It's what you do with the obstacle that creates strength, not what the obstacle does to you.

I trust myself. I trust my ability to overcome whatever obstacles I may face. I trust myself to bounce back stronger. My obstacles are pathways, not problems.

Jayde's Thoughts

What's an obstacle to someone who trusts themselves?
Still an obstacle. That belief that just makes getting in the ring to face it a little easier.

Obstacles show us that our tools are only sharpened by challenge and challenge requires you actually rolling up your sleeves and getting into the ring. There are many rings I climbed into just be dragged until the very last round when I finally found a way to win. There also many rings I stumbled into defeating whatever was in front of me 27 seconds into round one. Each fight showing me that even if an obstacle knocks me down, I'll keep getting back up and always find a way to win. These victories almost always then serve as the basic survival skills for the next level up.

Kellie's Thoughts

So the theme of this day was written well before finding the quote below and the alignment is remarkable. I find myself sitting, reflecting on everything and the person (s) that impersonated an obstacle in my life. Even those things which others believed were for my good, were truly impersonations of blindsided attacks. I didn't take it personal then and I still don't. WHY? Simply because with every obstacle a pound was added to this imaginary barbell (strong shoulders are beautiful lol). With each weight added, my strength and endurance improved. I wouldn't be half as strong today without the obstacles. And the scary truth: the weight is still being added and I am here for it. I have fully trusted myself to embrace the weight of obstacles, lift them up and keep lifting, because to whom much is given, much is required.

MY DAY EIGHTEEN

"Nothing stops the man who desires to achieve. Every obstacle is simply a course to develop his achievement muscle. It's a strengthening of his powers of accomplishment. "- Thomas Carlyle

---

DAY NINETEEN

Mediocrity may get you the car, but it won't provide the fuel.

I erase mediocrity from my vocabulary.

Jayde's Thoughts

I am terrified of squandering my gifts.

I have never wanted to live a small life. I am not moved by doing anything average. I've always known at my core, I was created to fulfill a purpose bigger than myself. And yet... I've still spent most of my life accepting and giving the bare minimum because it was the safe route. I spent years doing enough to get by instead of committing to excellence. I settled for just being invited to the table instead of using my voice to add value.

I've spent a lot of time asking myself "why?" and the only answer is fear. I've been afraid of dreaming too big in case my dreams didn't want me back. I trembled at the thought of asking for too much because I didn't know what I would do with it when I actually go it or if I was even worthy of it to begin with. I half-committed to doing the work because I feared I wasn't as great as I thought I was. I never woke up and said "I want to be mediocre," but my actions said it for me. Mediocrity is built from a series of decisions to keep playing small – and I've decided to stop playing small.

.

Kellie's Thoughts

I need to sit on this for a while. Mediocrity has been a major part of who I am and now I hear it lost its battle in my life. This is tragic. Who I have conditioned myself to be is now being ripped away. I never wanted to give too little or too much, just average. That mindset of being average made me walk away from great opportunities, neglect needed emotions, and settle for surface level possessions. I was good, I am good! At least, I thought I was until today.

Mediocrity has provided me a movement without a voice. Mediocrity has provided me a stage without an audience. Mediocrity has provided me a feast without an appetite. It's time to speak loud at the podium to people ready to listen. It's time to start eating good...mediocrity has been evicted! BossUp!

MY DAY NINETEEN

"There is always a heavy demand for fresh mediocrity. In every generation the least cultivated taste has the largest appetite." - Paul Gauguin

DAY TWENTY

Learn, grow, repeat.
I allow myself room to grow and the courage to start over.

Jayde's Thoughts
Growth is wild. You have these moments where you're in the thick of it and every moment is a fight to the bone to be and do better. Other times, there are a series of moments where you notice nothing. You're just going through the motions of your life, then BAM a moment comes where you realize you've grown beyond something that once held your world – and you can't remember when the switch flipped.

I exist a lot in the latter. I can't recall concrete growth spurts, but I can say that I've outgrown the life I once thought I wanted. In this moment, I no longer subscribe to a lot of the conventional things I once begged God for. I've gained new knowledge and let go of old programs and beliefs that no longer serve me. I've found that my wants and needs have evolved and I've grown out of my childhood dreams and catapulted into my purpose.

Kellie's Thoughts
Well, now that I have accepted the loss of my own mediocrity, I can begin to live and grow more effectively and purposefully. The metaphor of flowers and seasons come to mind. Like a flower, I have seasons of development and seasons of growth. I can no longer operate in full beast mode every season. I have learned that there are times to sit back and learn so that the right nourishment is poured into me for proper growth. It is okay to start over, beginnings can be tough, but also needed, And I will start over as many times as needed in order to learn and grow. The more I learn, the more I grow. The more I grow, the more I learn. It's a never-ending tune, my favorite song on repeat!

MY DAY TWENTY

"I keep turning over new leaves, and spoiling them, as I used to spoil my copybooks; and I make so many beginnings there never will be an end. (Jo March)" - Louisa May Alcott

_____

_____

_____

_____

_____

_____

_____

_____

_____

_____

_____

_____

_____

_____

DAY TWENTY-ONE

Trust the process and the space it provides you.
I am my own safe space. I am learning from this moment, there is good here.
I honor the space I am in.

Jayde's Thoughts
It is easier for me to lean into the process because I trust myself – and I trust God. I know God does not take us into relentless seas without the resources to make it safely to the shore. I also know I can fall down hard, but I know I can get back up because I've done it before. This does not mean I don't challenge or question or fight back during the process because I do. I just trust myself enough to move past those uncertainties on the journey.

I believe that God loves us too much to let us settle, so he shoves us into the uncomfortable and challenges us to really meet ourselves. Settling gets a lot harder to do when you've seen what you're capable of. Even when the process has me on the ropes and I'm ready to tap out, this belief keeps me in the ring. This unwavering belief also allows me to carve out my own path instead of choosing what is comfortable or fast or easy.

Kellie's Thoughts
If I cannot trust and appreciate the space I am in everyday, alone; then how can I expect anyone else to do the same. I believe that when you demonstrate unyielding appreciation to your space, people are forced to respect it or walk away. There is no room for judgement, just constructive criticism, which can at times be a hard pill to swallow. I am right where God wants me to be. God placed me in spaces that I never thought I would not be in; however, He orders my steps and for that, I am thankful. Every day I am reminded that God will take and plant me where I am needed, where I will grow, even when I don't believe it to be true. The process is full of ups and downs and I must be willing to honor whichever situation may occur.
I heard a saying, rather a question once that changed how I showed up in the process and the space it provided. "Are you leasing, renting, or owning your space". For so long I have been leasing and renting my space. My space was not my own. It's tough, but I have learned how to OWN my space and trust the process every day and know that platforms will present themselves to me when it is time!

MY DAY TWENTY-ONE

"Everybody wants the platform but nobody wants the process." - Pastor John Gray

DAY TWENTY-TWO

Empty out your thoughts and feelings.

I give myself permission to feel. I give myself permission to sit with my feelings and feel them in their entirety. I give myself the courage to be vulnerable. I recognize my feelings are my superpowers.
I divorce self-sabotage. I release the feelings that are not mine to hold.

Jayde's Thoughts

I've always been sensitive. I've just couldn't figure out how to use it as my superpower. I can't pinpoint the exact moments I started believing feelings were a sign of weakness, but I began tucking my sensitivity away in middle school. I taught myself that quick feet meant I could outrun unpleasant feelings. I dedicated my entire teen and adult life to running faster than my feelings could catch me. I just called it chasing adventure, so it sounded better. The funny thing about using adventure as a distraction is that eventually all the illusions have to fade.

You'll look up and the feelings you've been avoiding will still be right there – just patting the couch cushion, inviting you to take a seat. My failed attempts to outrun my feelings taught me that if you don't deal with them, no matter how fast you run or drive, they will deal with you. I've spent the last two years sitting with my feelings – and I've discovered they just needed room to be heard and felt fully without being shamed for existing.

Kellie's Thoughts

I just don't have time to interpret all these feelings. They lead to dead ends and I end up walking in a circle. The consequences, as always, of feelings and thoughts are just too hard to bare. So, I keep them locked up and throw away the key. You can't open what you don't have access too, right?! How do I feel? I feel numb, I feel nothing. Statements like "oh I feel you" has nothing to do with my emotions, just a means to support you [friends, family, etc.] while manipulating myself to feel something. A play own words have become my feelings, re-appropriating "feelings and thoughts" into something obscured, because honestly I can't face myself. I can't face the reality of what I truly feel. I can't empty out all this shit and still expect to be okay. If I empty out my thoughts and feelings, then what else do I have to control?! But if these feelings are meant to be given, I can't deny you that right – so here I go, learning to speak and express my feelings because tomorrow isn't promised. It still hurts like hell though...

MY DAY TWENTY-TWO

"Never be ashamed of what you feel. You have the right to feel any emotion that you want, and to do what makes you happy. That's my life motto" - Demi Lovato

DAY TWENTY-THREE

Honor your words and prepare for the manifestation.
I am my own answered prayers.

Jayde's Thoughts

Words have always been my place of refuge and my chosen medium. I believe words have power and the words we speak and write over our lives don't just stay words forever. I also believe that you get what you have the courage to ask for, that closed mouths won't ever be consistently fed, and anything can be a prayer if you're paying attention. I'm not just talking about the "God please see me to the other side of this darkness" kind of prayer either. I'm talking about the small conversations in everyday life, where nothing moves in the moment, but you walk away and nothing is really the same. Moments like:

- When something really amazing happens I whisper, "thank you, God. More please."
- When I'm in an intense growing season I repeat, "Thank you for the woman I grew out of, thank you for the woman I am, I look forward to the woman I'm becoming."
- When the only thing I can find to celebrate is me waking up that day I say, "I woke up today, that is enough."

There is nothing eloquent or flowery about these conversations, but they mean something. They heal, the activate magic, they keep me grounded.

Kellie's Thoughts

I pray often, I talk to God often. There is no set time, I just do it. I pray for people I know and people I will never meet. I pray for direction; I pray for healing. I just pray and talk all day long. What I have learned is that you have to be careful what you pray for, it just might be answered. And when I say that, I truly mean God will answer your prayer in one of two ways: answered without cost and answered with a cost. Regardless, it will be answered and that is a feeling that you must be ready to acknowledge and live with. I have accepted the fact that I MANIFEST – whew, I could tell you so many true stories! There is so much power in your words and you don't even realize it – it's scary. Its 2020 and everything I asked and prayed for in 2013 is rolling out as quick as the credits at the end of a movie (lol). I pray for clarity before I speak and manifest these days.

MY DAY TWENTY-THREE

"More tears are shed over answered prayers than unanswered ones" -Saint Teresa of Avila

_____

_____

_____

_____

_____

_____

_____

_____

_____

_____

_____

_____

_____

_____

_____

_____

_____

DAY TWENTY-FOUR

Love yourself no matter how difficult.

I love and accept myself fully for who I am right now.
I love myself enough to set boundaries and walk away when needed.
I love myself enough to take breaks when I need to.

Jayde's Thoughts

Here's how self-love has changed me:

I stopped questioning why God kept blessing me and realized I was worthy of every blessing that had ever been giftwrapped and left at my door. I stopped counting everyone who wasn't showing up for me and started standing in the front row of my own stadium tour giving my damn self a standing ovation. I gave myself room to make mistakes. I allowed myself to be seen and loved fully by someone else, knowing that their love didn't free from me the duty of loving myself first and most. I accepted that the life changing, mountain moving, earth shattering approval I had been craving, was really just my own. I stopped giving myself the bare minimum because I am worth more than just 20 minutes here and 15 minutes there.

Self-love made room for all of the selves in my life – self-compassion, self-grace, self-forgiveness. It made way for me to put myself first in a world that shames women for daring to put their own wants and needs at the top of their priority list. It made room for rest, for restoration, for joy. My own self-love taught me that me at my best, benefits the entire world.

Kellie's Thoughts

The hardest thing I had to face was loving the person I spent 24/7 with: myself. I mean truly fall in love because of who I am and not in spite of who I was, am, and will be. Like, how do you ask someone else "so tell me how to love myself". Sounds crazy right?! I was willing to do and try anything to say "I love me" and mean it! Self-help books, listening and watching inspirational videos, watching individuals who I thought loved themselves and then I tried to mimic them...all of that and it wasn't there. Why was it so hard to love myself? First of all, before you can love anything, you should try liking it first. That was it, I couldn't fully love myself because I didn't like myself. My looks, my attitude toward certain people and things, my career, my life. I just didn't like any of it. For every good thing that happen in my life there were about 3 bad things to follow. I was sick of it, literally! Somewhere, somehow, I started dating myself and it led to be liking myself – now I am in this loving and committed relationship with myself and no one can take that from me.

MY DAY TWENTY-FOUR
"Accept yourself, love yourself" - Chanel Iman

_____

_____

_____

_____

_____

_____

_____

_____

_____

_____

_____

_____

_____

_____

DAY TWENTY-FIVE

Eventually, you will have to release all the dreams you caught.

Everything I dream of is within reach. I was created to reach.
I divorce the idea that I need luck - my dreams have already been written in the stars.

Jayde's Thoughts

I'm writing today from a place of half liberation and half being scared shitless. I recently walked away from the job I used to pray for to take an entry level position in a new field. I landed my dream job at 26 doing work I convinced myself I was put on earth to do, only to spend every day thinking "I just thought it would feel better than this." I started to think that maybe God just had a sense of humor – sometimes giving us everything we thought we wanted, just to show us that we didn't really want it after all.

Maybe my dreams didn't completely change though, maybe I just finally grew tired from chasing all the things other people told me I should want. Maybe I've finally gotten fed up with adopting other people's dreams as my own. Maybe I just finally choose me – and choose beginning again over staying in a dream that just isn't mine. I think we do ourselves a disservice by holding on to all the things not meant for us, especially in the times we continue to clutch tightly things when everything inside of us is screaming for us to let go. Besides, if our hands are bloody from holding on to all the things not meant for us, we'll stain every new gift trying to unwrap itself in our laps.

Kellie's Thoughts

Whew, this affirmation is right on time today. As I read an email full of opportunities that I once only dreamed about. It had nothing to do with luck, just hard work being seen by others, that I never met. Every day I yearn for the night to get away from my reality and dream of a different reality. Some dreams, I admit are far-fetched, but they are mine and make me feel good if only during 6 hours of sleep. However, today, I broke down what a dream means for me: **Destined to Reach Elevate And Manifest**. My eyes allow me to see beyond my situation. My legs and feet allow me to walk paths unknown and sometimes bare the strength to stand alone. My arms provide the needed length to allow my hands to grab each dream. Because of who I am, I know I was created to reach my dreams. Because of who I will be, I have the courage to release my dreams and watch my reality transform as do the stars above.

MY DAY TWENTY-FIVE

"The biggest adventure you can take is to live the life of your dreams" - Oprah Winfrey

_____

_____

_____

_____

_____

_____

_____

_____

_____

_____

_____

_____

_____

_____

_____

DAY TWENTY-SIX

Lift as you climb.

There is a blessing in the pressing. I am a magnet for authentic connection.

Jayde's Thoughts

I don't believe meaningful success can come to fruition without some sort of village. I consider myself to be independent, and yet there is nothing meaningful I've achieved on my own. Behind every milestone I've reached has been family covering me in prayer, behind every award there's been friends reminding me I could do challenging things, and behind every leap of faith there's been a network helping me master skills to land on my feet.

We lift as we climb because concrete walls are easier to break through with help. We lift as we climb because there's always a seat at our table for those doing the work. We lift as we climb because there's always room in our community for new tables to be built. We lift as we climb because we've been lifted as we've climbed. We lift as we climb because of the giants we know who chose to make space for collaboration rather than making us feel small on our journeys.

Kellie's Thoughts

So, remember back on day 6, I set my first therapy appointment? Well, today was the day. It was great and I wish I would have done it a long time ago. Long story short, therapy is worth the price! So, back to today, this affirmation will always speak volumes to me and my life. I am immediately reminded of the words written in Galatians 6:9, where in due season we shall reap what we have sown, if we faint not. Everything that I been through (voluntarily and involuntarily) served a purpose in my life. It was all worth the tears, because I am stronger and more willing and ready to walk in my purpose with my head held high. I use my story as a testimony to overcoming life's many obstacles that are created to keep us falling, broken, and stumbling along the path. My pressing is part of my blessing and because of that I am available to lift others up as I climb!

MY DAY TWENTY-SIX

"Once you make it to your point of making it, you'll appreciate the struggle" - Nas

DAY TWENTY-SEVEN

Just show up.
I am exactly where I need to be. Even when it doesn't feel like it.
I will show up for myself.

Jayde's Thoughts
There is an art to just showing up.
For yourself. For your loved ones. For the work.
Showing up to be seen fully and heard in totality.
Even if it's a fight to the bone to do so.

Showing up is a rebellion against the voices telling me I can't.
It's a declaration to be present for myself and the world.
It's a sacred pact with God, with myself, with my purpose.
It's a belief that as I continue showing up, miracles will multiply on my behalf.

Kellie's Thoughts
I make no more apologies for how and when I show up. I am invested in showing up unapologetically and authentically with an array of intelligence dripping down my presence. What and who doesn't respect me, is not my problem. My ability to sit, kneel, and stand for justice and anything else I support, for that matter, is beyond a right or privilege, it is my legacy...it is my purpose. As soon as I walk through the door, I know that I already achieved 80% of the success I deserve and demand. Good, bad, and indifferent 0 there are still days I have; however, my fire will never cease. When I don't feel like showing up, I remind myself of what it means to others when I don't show up.
Zora Neale Hurston said it best "Those that don't got it, can't show it. Those that got it, can't hide it." and "Sometimes, I feel *discriminated against,* but it does not make me angry. It merely astonishes me. How can any deny themselves the *pleasure of my company*? It's beyond me."

MY DAY TWENTY-SEVEN
"Eighty percent of success is showing up" - Woody Allen

_____

_____

_____

_____

_____

_____

_____

_____

_____

_____

_____

_____

_____

_____

_____

_____

DAY TWENTY-EIGHT

The right kind of no is better than the wrong kind of yes.

I divorce being a people pleaser. I release the need to say "yes" when I really mean "no." I free myself from the need to explain my "no."
I welcome challenges, even if it means saying "NO".

Jayde's Thoughts

We often hear about the "yes" that shifts things for our favorite artists, musicians, writers, and entrepreneurs. We then spend so much of our lives searching for or own "yes," that we forget how important the "no's" are too. I don't just mean the rejections we all hear related to our dreams and passions, I'm not just talking about the wave of insecurity that comes from wanting someone who didn't want us back, and I don't just mean the breaks that didn't go our way either. I mean the "no's" we tell other people and the "no's" that serve us because "no" isn't just a momentary disappointment, it's also:

- a boundary – and boundaries keep our values intact
- an energy conserver – so we can focus on what's really important to us
- protection – from doors and opportunities that take us further off our paths in the long run
- redirection – to the right opportunity and moment

Now.. I can admit I've never met a "no" that felt good, but they've always been necessary – and they've always led to something much better.

Kellie's Thoughts

I said what I said, now watch me work! I have realized through these past 28 days that a delay is not a denial and that some "NO's" are good for you. Now, before these 28 days, life was a little different. I gave everything of myself to others. Wanting to please them because I had to feel needed. So I spent more moments being a "YES GIRL" than a "let me check my self-care meter first". The ability to say "NO" despite the desire to say "YES" is growth, and for me it was a significant milestone in womanhood. I seriously thought I was doing the right thing. People needed me and I had the money, time, etc. to assist, so I did. I never wanted anything in return. Then I noticed that even with giving to others, I was taking from myself. My self-care was non-existent at age 32 and everything about my life had a foundation in someone else. This wasn't the life I needed and soon learned, it wasn't the life I wanted anymore. I had

to take my life back and love on me a little longer. So, I read a book by
Shonda Rhimes "Year of Yes" and her story spoke to my situation.
Sometimes to get clarity you have to view it from another person's perspective
– just don't rest too long in their perspective (lol).

MY DAY TWENTY-EIGHT
"Losing yourself does not happen all at once. Losing yourself happens one no at a time." - Shonda Rhimes

_____

_____

_____

_____

_____

_____

_____

_____

_____

_____

_____

_____

_____

DAY TWENTY-NINE

Sound your trumpet.

I am brilliant. I am walking magic. I am loved.
I free myself from the idea that I need other people to see my vision. I free
myself from valuing someone else's opinions over my own.

Jayde's Thoughts

There is nothing to be gained from downplaying your achievements in an
attempt to be described as humble. Your network can't open doors if they
don't know what your passions are. People can't put you on when you're quiet
about your talents. And opportunities to grow can't find you when you're
hiding. I know society loves a humble brag, but the greats taught us to
proclaim our greatness and be seen. The world will not wake up to give you
your flowers until you're already swimming in your own garden. Other people
being uncomfortable with you loving yourself out loud isn't your problem.
You have to celebrate you until the world catches on – celebration does not
require shrinkage or light dimming.

Kellie's Thoughts

You know what's crazy, today at work each person I spoke too began to speak
of my talents and potential, and singing my praises. And here I was listening
but not moving to the beat of their singing. Then to have this affirmation on
today, God knows! I have always walked around with a song in my head.
Someone else's beat, melody, and words about my life has been on constant
repeat. And while I appreciate it, it is time I create my own sound that
embodies my vision, truth, and self-worth. It's time to write my own song. I
must recognize my own strengths and overdone strengths (I release the
mindset of weaknesses) and learn to work within them and not in spite of
them. After saying all that, I am sitting here trying to figure out what sound
will come from my trumpet: smooth 90s, ol' school hip hop, new age country,
or foot stomping gospel. There must be a balance of pride and humility in the
sound as well. Regardless, I am ready to own my space and groove with my
beat to life!

MY DAY TWENTY-NINE

"If you don't toot your own horn, you can't enjoy the music." - Debbie Allen

DAY THIRTY

When it is all said and done, the greatest decision made was my most defining moment in life.

I choose myself. I am a magnet for abundance and welcome it in all forms.

Jayde's Thoughts
Day 30. I made it. You made it. We made it.

Defining moments don't always come with a blow horn and confetti – sometimes they are quiet glimpses of clarity on your commute to work or in the bathroom. Sometimes they're small, seemingly insignificant decisions we make to reclaim and walk in our power. That's the truth that makes sense for me at this point in my journey at least. I didn't have this big "AHA" moment where I strutted into my purpose, instead I stumbled into it by making one decision at a time to choose myself. One decision to bet on myself and to continue showing up for myself. And even when my hands trembled and voice cracked, I chose myself anyway.

My hope is that on the last day of this journey, you'll find new ways to shake free from fear and choose yourself too. That you won't let the work intimidate you or the times you feel unsure of what's next swallow you whole. But most importantly, I hope that you will keep on showing up, speaking positive affirmations over your life (reclaiming them when you must), and betting on yourself. Even when it's not the quick or easy thing to do. Even when fear is loud and imposter syndrome suits up for a battle you're tired of fighting. My commitment to myself today, is to continue to do the same for me.

Kellie's Thoughts
Day 30! Here is the thing, I battle with expressing my emotions and at one point had suicidal thoughts. I tend to be lonely in a crowd and at times voiceless near a mic. I don't have it all together despite what others may think, but that's the great part about my life's journey - It is my adventure.

I make no apologies for who I am. I have spent the last 30 days reflecting on myself and avoiding this moment, this vulnerability of talking about me and breaking me apart – exposing myself to strangers! I am thankful that you went on the 30-day journey with me, I didn't have to do this alone. You made this possible for me. You allowed me the space to be transparent. You made me realize that someone else will benefit from me choosing myself, finally!
YOU ARE WORTH THE INVESTMENT!

MY DAY THIRTY

"What you get is what you see and I bring me" -Lyrics from *I Bring Me* by the cast of Star

_____

_____

_____

_____

_____

_____

_____

_____

_____

_____

_____

_____

_____

_____

_____

30-Day Affirmation List

Day 1: **Acknowledge the work to be done and do it.**
- I am committed to doing the work.
- I know the work will not always be pretty or fun and still choose to do it anyway.
- I know that everything begins and ends with doing the work.

Day 2: **Self-discipline is the first step.**
- I have the discipline, patience, and passion to achieve all of my goals.
- My dreams are already my reality.
- I divorce self-sabotage.

Day 3: **You can change the perception about yourself.**
- Life is for me.
- All things work on my behalf.
- I've already won.
- I free myself from creating barriers to my own success.

Day 4: **You aren't lost, stop finding yourself and start appreciating yourself.**
- I am my own answered prayers.
- I already am everything I want.

Day 5: **Competency is not about age, yet experiences.**
- I have all I need in this moment; God has equipped me with all that I need.
- I am wise enough, smart enough, and strong enough to do this.
- I deserve to be here in this space.
- I deserve all of the abundance in my life.

Day 6: **Be genuine in your need, ask for help.**
- I trust myself and God to have my back.
- I recognize I don't have to do it all alone because I have a community that wants to see me succeed.

Day 7: **Too many people will cause self-neglect if you aren't careful.**
- I am at the top of my priority list.
- I am enough on my own.
- I recognize I cannot be everything to everyone and I free myself from any guilt or shame that comes with that.

Day 8: **Others expectations of me don't fit my experiences. Live life!**
- I free myself from the expectations others have placed on me.
- I give myself permission to grow beyond the boxes other people have put me in.
- I recognize that I am not the expectations I fall short of.

Day 9: **People will remix your life and never give recognition to the original.**
- I recognize that my life is magic.
- I am the secret ingredient; I am the magic touch.

Day 10: **Regroup and refocus.**
- I free myself from the relationships, environments, and beliefs that no longer serve me.
- I give myself permission to grow beyond the boxes other people have put me in.

Day 11: **Every day is an opportunity. You decide whether it will be bad or good.**
- I divorce the idea that I am unworthy of love.
- I create sunshine wherever I go.
- I have the power to create the life I want.

Day 12: **This moment is all there is. Own it.**
- I give myself permission to acknowledge my fears; I am courageous enough to face them head on.

Day 13: **Move now, later may never come.**
- I deserve to be here in this space. I deserve all of the abundance in my life.

Day 14: **I don't have to be perfect.**
- I free myself from the thought that I have to perform in order to be loved.
- I know that I am enough on my own.
- I release the fear of being judged for being me.

Day 15: **Be better than the person you were yesterday, that's your only competition.**
- Greatness has been in me all along.

Day 16: **Remember, it's a marathon, not a sprint.**
- I recognize my power and I am ready to fully walk in it.

Day 17: **As long as you are moving, you are taking the next step.**
- I divorce the idea that I have to settle.
- The importance of taking small steps

Day 18: **It's what you do with the obstacle that creates strength, not what the obstacle does to you.**
- I trust myself.
- I trust my ability to overcome whatever obstacles I face.
- I trust myself to bounce back stronger.
- I recognize my obstacles as pathways, not problems.

Day 19: **Mediocrity may get you the car, but it won't provide the fuel.**
- I erase mediocrity from my vocabulary.

Day 20: **Learn, grow, repeat.**
- I allow myself room to grow and the courage to start over.

Day 21: **Trust the process and the space it provides you.**
- I am my own safe space.
- There is good in this moment.
- I honor the space I am in.

Day 22: **Empty out your thoughts and feelings.**
- I give myself permission to sit with my feelings and feel them in their entirety.
- I give myself the courage to be vulnerable.
- I recognize that my feelings are my superpowers.
- I release the feelings that are not my own to hold.

Day 23: **Honor your words and prepare for the manifestation.**
- I am my own answered prayers.

Day 24: **Love yourself no matter how difficult.**
- I love and accept myself fully for who I am right now.
- I love myself enough to set boundaries and walk away when needed.
- I love myself enough to take breaks when I need to.

Day 25: **Eventually, you will have to release all the dreams you caught.**
- Everything I dream of is within reach.
- I was created to reach.
- I divorce the idea that I need luck - my dreams have already been written in the stars.

Day 26: **Life as you climb.**
- There is a blessing in the pressing.

Day 27: **Just show up.**
- I am exactly where I need to be – even when it doesn't feel like it.
- I will show up for myself.

Day 28: **The right kind of "no" is better than the wrong kind of "yes."**
- I divorce being a people pleaser. I release the need to say "yes" when I really mean "no.
- I free myself from the need to explain my "no."
- I say "YES" to challenges, even if it means saying "NO".

Day 29: **Sound your trumpet.**
- I am brilliant. I am walking magic. I am loved.
- I free myself from the idea that I need other people to see my vision.
- I free myself from valuing someone else's opinions over my own.
- I deserve to be here in this space. I deserve all of the abundance in my life.

Day 30: **When it is all said and done, the greatest decision made was my most defining moment in life.**
- I choose myself.
- I free myself from needing someone else to recognize my talents.

Acknowledgements

From Jayde:

This book exists in the world with much appreciation to:

Lelia Mae + Alma Louise: Thank you for passing your freckles and fearless approach to life down to me.

Emmanuel Harris: Your faith alone has always been strong enough for the both of us.

Robin Becker + Dale Ware: All that is my life is because of your love and unwavering support of me. Thank you for letting me do life on my terms.

My brothers: I believe in each of your dreams as fiercely as my own. Aden, you are my hero.

& to those who continue to share laughter with me on this journey: You know who you are. I started writing again because you reminded me we shouldn't give up on our gifts.

From Kellie (Dr. K):

Thank you to my colleague, Dr. Lundy, for providing a thought-provoking foreword. Thank you to my dear friend and motivator, Queen, for conducting such an inspiring and timely interview with Jayde and I. Additionally, I acknowledge every individual that offered a piece of their space to me, for me to just be me! The tears, the laughter, the conversations that continue to help us be better versions of ourselves – because we need that space now more than ever.

To *Love*, thank you for reminding me that I deserve happiness and capable of giving it to others despite what I think my situations may look like. Thank you for reassuring me how powerful my words are towards manifestation.

by Black Women

It's important that we highlight the Black women who helped make this book possible. The introduction, the foreword, and the book cover are all by Black women. – Thank You

Notes/References

Notes/References

About the Writer of the Foreword – Dr. Rae Lundy

Dr. Raé N. Lundy is a licensed clinical psychologist, mental health activist, TEDx Speaker, and the Associate Vice President for Student Health, Counseling, and Wellness at Wiley College. Her mission is to improve psychological health and wellbeing within communities of color by engaging in honest conversations about self-care, fostering healing dialogue, and reducing mental health stigma.

Recognized for providing culturally competent and inclusive psychological support, Dr. Lundy is particularly skilled in serving the needs of Black and underserved students through clinical counseling, training, advocacy, coalition building, educational instruction, and research.

Dr. Lundy serves on several boards most notably *StandUp SpeakOut*, a national nonprofit created to support survivors of trauma.

See her in action: View Dr. Lundy's TEDx Talk focused on self-care and mental wellness.

About the Writer of the Introduction – Queen-Ella Pringle

Queen-Ella Renee Pringle emerged from New York City and discovered her independence in Atlanta Georgia, where she began to make a difference in the lives of those she touched. She later joined the United States Air Force. As a military member, she worked in a profession where human relations and leadership was part of her everyday interactions with local and foreign officials addressing concerns and providing assistance for effective resolutions.

Being led by spiritual guidance and intuition has led to extraordinary experiences in ministry, consulting, coaching, professional, and personal development. Her specialty areas include maternal care coaching, empowerment coaching, purposeful living, youth/adult coaching, and family coaching.

Queen-Ella Renee obtained her B.A. in Criminal Justice from Columbia Southern University in 2010 while serving in the military and being stationed abroad. With her strong desire to make an impact on the lives of others, she later completed her M.A. in Human Services Counseling with a focus in Marriage and Family from Liberty University. June 2018 is when she had a strong desire to culminate her skills and officially begin serving God by serving others. With this, she birthed Cornerstone Visionaries Consulting & Coaching which provides service to youth, adults, and families in growth and development.

She has extensive experience working with military service members and their families and is currently employed by the United States Air Force as the Exceptional Family Member Program Family Support Coordinator. In this capacity she oversees 600 families who have special needs providing resources, empowerment support, and consultation for service providers and families.

Queen-Ella is a proud mother to Gabriella and Quincy. She is a member of Zeta Phi Beta Sorority, Inc.

She is the author of Unlocking Your Womanhood: Five Domains to Developing and Practicing Spiritual Self-Care through Adversity – coming August 2020.

Queen-Ella can be contacted at cornerstonevisionaries@gmail.com.

About the Author

Jayde Ware

Jayde Ware is an alumna of Longwood University where she obtained a Bachelor's of Science degree in Therapeutic Recreation. Jayde is a writer, content creator, facilitator, and full-time student affairs professional. She is a woman of many passions and interests, but specializes in facilitating conversations that matter and creating content that connects. She is deeply committed to risk prevention work, wellness, and community building.

Above all of her titles, Jayde considers herself a creative first and strongly believes in the power of storytelling as a means for genuine human connection. She is a fierce advocate for moisturizing often and minding one's own business as a daily act. Jayde is a native of Virginia, but she has dedicated her life to moving often – creating home wherever her purpose leads.

In her personal life, Jayde loves reading, tweeting through life, and arguing about her sports takes. She is a proud member of Zeta Phi Beta Sorority, Inc.

You can keep up with Jayde via twitter (@astoldbyjayde) and Instagram (@callherjayde).

About the Author

Dr. Kellie M. Dixon (Dr. K)

Dr. Kellie M. Dixon received an Associate of Science degree in Science from Danville Community College, a Bachelor of Science degree in Kinesiology and Master of Science degree in Community and College Counseling from Longwood University. In addition, she received a doctorate from Grand Canyon University in Organizational Leadership with an emphasis in Organizational Development.

Dr. Dixon is a Certified Life Coach through the Life Coach Institute of Orange County. As a well-respected and sought after consultant, life coach, and mentor, Dr. Dixon is committed to the holistic well-being and achievement of both individuals and organizations. She is well-known for her commitment to the progression and experiences of both students and faculty/staff at HBCUs through her work in institutional effectiveness (i.e. accreditation and assessment) and staff development. She is the author of Recharge: A Self Awareness Approach to Goal Achievement.

A Virginia, back roads, country native, Dr. Dixon is the founder of Clear Pathway Consulting Services, LLC, where she uses her passion for helping others through holistic wellness coaching, higher education consulting, and career coaching. Dr. Dixon is a well-respected colleague in higher education. When she's not coaching, consulting, or mentoring, Dr. Dixon enjoys listening/dancing to music, traveling, and spending time with family, friends, loved ones, and her four-legged son, Kofi. She is a proud member of Zeta Phi Beta Sorority, Inc.

You can keep up with Dr. K via twitter (@misskellie and @clearpathway).

Made in the USA
Columbia, SC
28 June 2022